SCIENTISTS
IN THE FIELD

ASTRONOMERS

Tom Greve

Rourke
Educational Media

rourkeeducationalmedia.com

Before Reading:

Building Academic Vocabulary and Background Knowledge

Before reading a book, it is important to tap into what your child or students already know about the topic. This will help them develop their vocabulary, increase their reading comprehension, and make connections across the curriculum.

1. *Look at the cover of the book. What will this book be about?*
2. *What do you already know about the topic?*
3. *Let's study the Table of Contents. What will you learn about in the book's chapters?*
4. *What would you like to learn about this topic? Do you think you might learn about it from this book? Why or why not?*
5. *Use a reading journal to write about your knowledge of this topic. Record what you already know about the topic and what you hope to learn about the topic.*
6. *Read the book.*
7. *In your reading journal, record what you learned about the topic and your response to the book.*
8. *After reading the book complete the activities below.*

Content Area Vocabulary
Read the list. What do these words mean?

asteroid
astronaut
atmosphere
elliptical
engineering
hypothesis
infinite
infrared
irresistible
mathematician
observational
physical
physics

After Reading:

Comprehension and Extension Activity

After reading the book, work on the following questions with your child or students in order to check their level of reading comprehension and content mastery.

1. *Why is Earth's atmosphere so important to life on this planet? (Asking questions)*
2. *Why has our view of the solar system changed over time? (Infer)*
3. *Explain what the night sky looks like in a populated area versus a rural area. What affects your view of the night sky in your area? (Text to self connection)*
4. *How are amateurs helping the field of astronomy? (Summarize)*
5. *How does the author help you visualize what space looks like? (Visualize)*

Extension Activity

A constellation is a group of stars that forms a pattern in the sky. Astrologists believe the stars and planets influence a person's life. Astrologists use zodiac signs, which are constellations associated with a person's birthday. Look up your zodiac sign. What constellation represents you? What characteristics and traits are associated with that sign? Does it sound like you? Try it out with a friend or family member. Do they match their zodiac sign?

TABLE OF CONTENTS

EYES TO THE SKIES

As long as people have been on Earth, they have stared with wild wonder into the night sky. What is out there? Why are the stars twinkling? How far away is the Moon?

Human understanding of the Moon, stars, and worlds beyond our own has grown by leaps and bounds over just the past few generations.

Stars are so far from Earth that their light is distorted by Earth's atmosphere and they sometimes appear to twinkle. Visible planets, such as Venus, do not twinkle because they are much closer.

Most astronomers concentrate on a particular question or area of astronomy: planetary science, solar astronomy, the origin or evolution of stars, or the formation of galaxies. Observational astronomers spend their time designing and carrying out observational programs with a telescope to answer a question or test the predictions of theories.

The universe beyond our planet is limitless. So are the mysteries hiding within its cold, dark void.

Over centuries, scientific minds have used their own observation, and, more recently, stunning advances in technology, to pull back the curtain on just a tiny fraction of the endless unknowns of outer space.

Giant telescopes housed in observatories act as a kind of window to the stars. Many observatories are built in remote locations at high altitudes.

Observatory on Mauna Kea, Hawaii

SUN

Venus

Earth

Mercury

Mars

Earth is one of eight planets in our solar system. Astronomers call the four nearest the Sun the rocky planets. The four farthest from the Sun are called the gas giants.

Those who study space, the planets and stars, and the **infinite** realms beyond our own solar system are astronomers. They play an important role in understanding our Earth, and its place in a universe so vast, it can sometimes defy our understanding.

Astronomy is a **physical** science. While life sciences such as biology are more concerned with the study of living things, astronomers study the physical makeup and activity of objects in space.

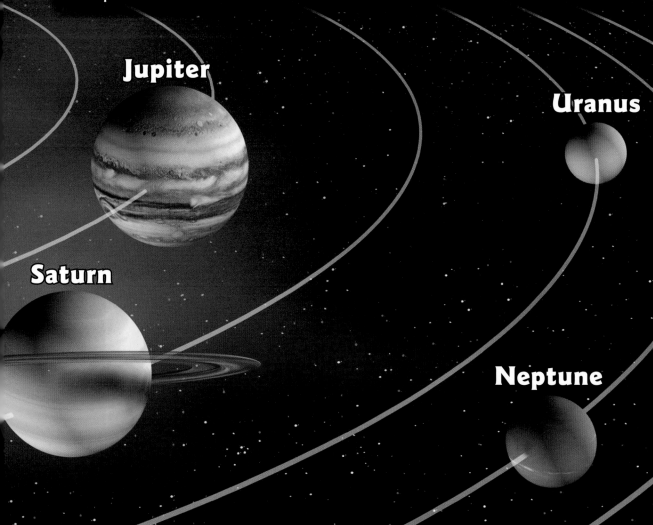

Jupiter

Uranus

Saturn

Neptune

The scientific knowledge we have about our planet Earth, its Moon, other planets in our solar system, asteroids, the Milky Way **galaxy**, and the infinite number of galaxies beyond it, is based on the work of astronomers.

Thanks to gravity, our Sun, which is really a medium-sized star, holds eight planets and other objects in orbit. But there are countless other suns and solar systems in our galaxy, and there are countless other galaxies beyond our own. This infinite expanse makes up the universe, or the **cosmos**.

Astronomers believe there are billions of solar systems beyond our own. That means Earth is like a grain of sand on an entire beach of planets, moons, and stars.

If a person could stand on a planet in another galaxy and identify Earth's solar system in the sky, it would appear as nothing more than a tiny speck of light, just like the tens of thousands of specks of light we can see from Earth on a clear night.

FIELD NOTES

The time astronomers spend at a telescope collecting data for analysis is only the beginning. Most of their time is spent in an office analyzing data, creating computer programs that allow them to more efficiently search through the data, writing research papers, and attending meetings.

Astronomy research shows that the order of the objects in outer space, our planet orbiting around our Sun, and countless other planets orbiting around countless other suns, are all a result of the forces of gravity, and time.

Gravity and time are **irresistible** forces. They rule life on Earth and they maintain order of our solar system and the universe.

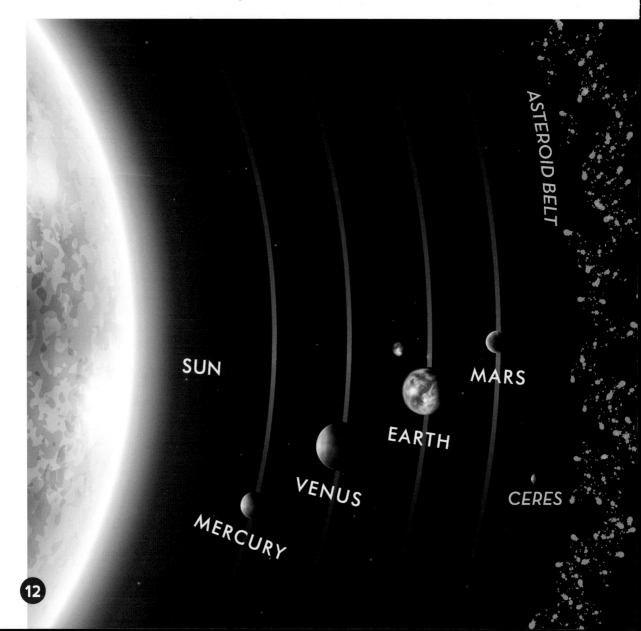

SUN

MARS

EARTH

VENUS

CERES

MERCURY

ASTEROID BELT

Same force, different scale: no matter how hard somebody throws or kicks a ball, the force of gravity will always cause it to land on the ground. Gravity also keeps the Sun, stars, moons, and planets in their places.

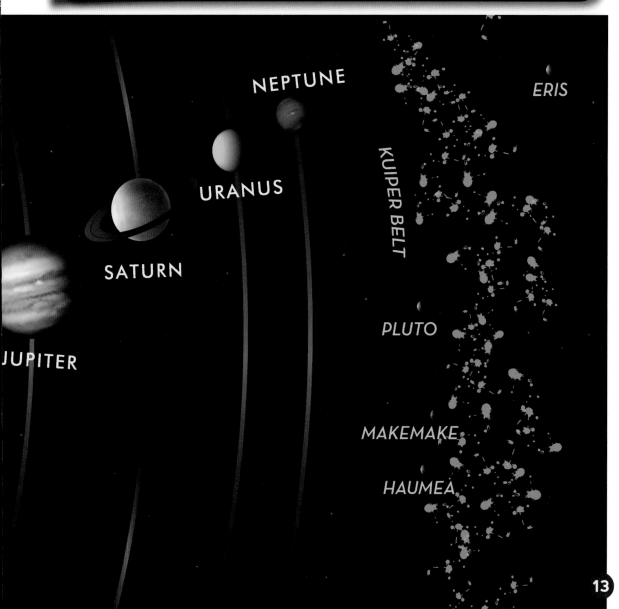

NEPTUNE

ERIS

URANUS

KUIPER BELT

SATURN

PLUTO

JUPITER

MAKEMAKE

HAUMEA

Like dust and dirt can collect and form dust bunnies in a corner of a room, dust particles in space gather and snowball into a star, a planet, or an **asteroid**. This is the work of gravity through time.

Because of gravity, the universe is a series of spinning bodies in motion, each body orbiting around something else in a dizzying dance of circular motion.

ASTROLOGY vs ASTRONOMY

The place of the Sun, Moon, and stars in the sky has given humans a way to mark the passing of seasons and time. An astronomer is a scientist who studies the **physics** of these objects. An astrologer is a person who thinks there are connections between the alignment of stars and planets in space, and events in people's lives here on Earth.

A horoscope is for astrology. A telescope is for astronomy.

Astronomy is an area of science that captures imaginations with out-of-this-world questions that many struggle to understand. The nature of an endless universe boggles the mind. Modern astronomy allows people to see places no human can ever expect to touch, at distances no human could ever expect to travel. It also begs the question: Could there be life on another planet?

Astronomers can identify features of planets from distant galaxies. One planet, named Kepler 186f, is thought to be like Earth in terms of size and distance from its sun. This leads some scientists to theorize that it might support life, even though its sun is smaller and dimmer than our own.

Nicolaus Copernicus

1473-1543

Polish astronomer and **mathematician** Nicolaus Copernicus developed a theory that the Earth was not the center of the universe. He correctly described the Sun as the object the Earth orbits around. This idea, while true, upset many people of his time because it contradicted religious understanding of the Earth.

The Copernican model of the Sun-centered solar system also showed other planets such as Venus and Mars orbiting the Sun at different speeds than Earth. This is why, when Venus and Earth are close, Venus appears brighter. As Venus moves ahead in its faster orbit, it grows dim because of its distance.

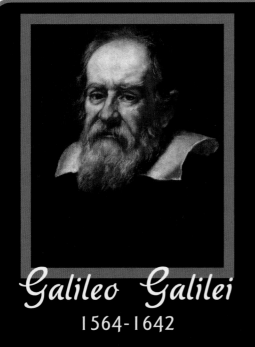

Galileo Galilei
1564-1642

Italian scientist Galileo Galilei was the first astronomer to use a telescope to observe space. Galileo is considered the father of **observational** astronomy. His observations and understanding of the solar system was far ahead of his time. He also designed and built his own telescopes to see farther into space than ever before. His observations through his telescopes not only proved the Copernican theory of the Sun as the center of the solar system, but also documented physical features such as craters on the surface of the Moon. He was also the first to see and prove that multiple moons orbit the planet Jupiter.

Renaissance Men

Copernicus and Galileo were both products of the Renaissance. It was a historic time between the 14th and 17th centuries when humans made great progress in scientific and artistic understanding. In many ways, the increased reliance on science to understand the physical world during the Renaissance helped move humans from the Dark Ages to modern times.

A Matter of Perspective

Before Galileo, and even somewhat after, it was hard for most humans to imagine that Earth moved around the Sun. To the naked eye, it can seem like everything in the sky is moving except the Earth.

Modern astronomy research and the technologies that support it are beyond anything Galileo or his fellow scientists could have likely imagined.

Though people still use smaller personal telescopes, astronomy research often involves larger interactive educational telescopes, such as the Goldstone-Apple Valley Radio Telescope in California. Viewing space through a telescope is better at night, away from the reflected lights of cities.

The mysterious depths of the universe and its endless assortment of galaxies, stars, planets, and moons, means no matter how much we discover, there will be new mysteries created at the same time. That is good news for young people intrigued by astronomy. Chances are, there will always be mysteries to solve in a universe we cannot fully fathom.

In 2012, astronomers announced they found three small rocky planets, all smaller than Earth, in tight orbits around a dwarf, or very small, star in a distant part of the galaxy. The star is known as KOI-196. Its planets are so close, they each orbit around it in less than two days. It is the smallest solar system discovered by astronomers.

THE CURIOUS CASE OF PLUTO

Generations of people have understood Earth's solar system to have one Sun and nine planets. The ninth and final planet, the one farthest from the Sun, was Pluto.

OUR SOLAR SYSTEM

SUN Mercury Venus Earth Mars

In addition to having such a relatively large moon, researchers also knew Pluto's orbit around the Sun was oddly **elliptical** versus the other planets. By the 1990s, researchers formed a **hypothesis** that there may be gravitational pull on Pluto from other objects in its astronomical neighborhood on the far edge of our solar system.

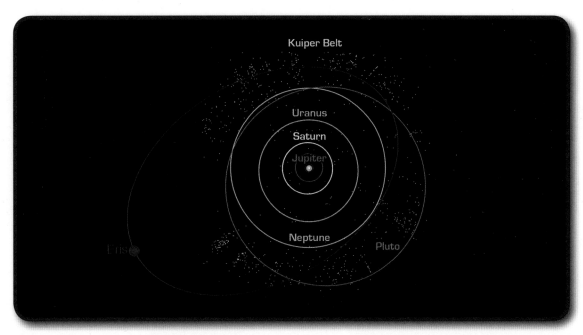

By 1992, researchers began spotting other objects near Pluto. The presence of the objects, in what astronomers called the Kuiper Belt, was evidence that Pluto may not be a planet in the same sense as the other eight. Thirteen years later, researchers discovered a Kuiper Belt object even larger than Pluto. They named it Eris.

Finally in 2006, at a meeting of the International Astronomical Union, after a heated debate over the astronomical definition of just what makes something a planet, Pluto was reclassified as a dwarf planet. It was a sibling, of sorts, to Eris, but did not possess the same astronomical characteristics of the other eight planets.

Much, but certainly not all, of the research that took us from discovering Pluto, to calling it a planet for nearly 80 years, to now calling it a dwarf planet, involved research using telescopes of various designs, functions, and specialties.

Astronomers have identified and named five dwarf planets in our solar system. Each is far smaller than Earth; in fact, they are even smaller than Earth's Moon.

Haumea

Makemake

Earth's Moon

Eris

Ceres

Pluto

Jocelyn Bell
Burnell
1943-

Jocelyn Bell Burnell is an astronomy researcher who discovered pulsars, or the radioactive pulses of light sent off by dead stars. She helped the International Astronomical Union reach its decision to reclassify Pluto as a dwarf planet.

But unlike Galileo and astronomers from previous generations, researchers now spend little time staring into space with a telescope. When they do observe outer space, they typically do it using a highly complex and powerful remote-operated telescope while sitting at a computer. They might even do it from home.

In addition to being curious about objects in the universe, astronomers need to be proficient in mathematics. Performing astronomy research without doing math is a little like trying to plant a garden without touching the soil.

MIND-BLOWING MATH AND FREAKY PHYSICS

Sir Isaac Newton

1643-1727

Sir Isaac Newton was born the same year Galileo died. Newton expanded on Galileo's findings in astronomy and super-charged them with math and physics. According to legend, Newton saw an apple fall from a tree and began to theorize that the gravitational force that brought down the apple extended beyond Earth. Eventually Newton put forth his three laws of motion and the theory that gravity dictates all movement, including the movement of objects in outer space.

"If I have seen further, it is by standing on the shoulders of giants." –Sir Isaac Newton

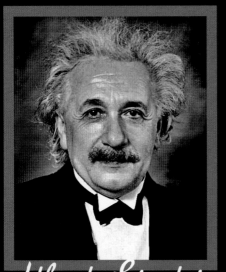

Albert Einstein

1879-1955

Albert Einstein had wild hair and even wilder intelligence. Though he was not technically an astronomer, he changed astronomy with his theory of relativity. The theory explained the laws of physics apply everywhere in the universe, not just on Earth. He created a mathematical model to explain that matter and energy are the same thing, and that light moves at a constant speed of 186,000 miles (299 kilometers) per second. His equation, $E = mc^2$, has become part of basic astronomy, and even part of popular culture, even though most people don't fully understand it.

The discoveries of Newton and Einstein propelled physics and astronomy. Newton's quote about standing on the shoulders of giants suggests that advances in scientific knowledge come about thanks to discoveries made in the past.

THE APOLLO PROGRAM: NASA'S FREAKIEST FEAT OF PHYSICS

In August of 1969, the National Aeronautics and Space Administration (NASA) did more than observe an astronomical object. They went to one.

Astronauts Neil Armstrong and Buzz Aldrin rocketed to the Moon, walked on its surface, and returned to Earth. The amount of science and **engineering** that went into the Apollo Space Program, and its successful exploration of the Moon, makes it one of the greatest achievements in the history of humanity.

Neil Armstrong spent about two and a half hours outside the spacecraft, Aldrin spent slightly less, and together they collected 47.5 pounds (21.5 kilograms) of lunar material to return to Earth.

If Venus and Mars are Earth's neighbors, then the Moon is more like Earth's garage, or its backyard. It is about 239,000 miles (384,000 kilometers) from Earth. That is a long distance if you have to take a car, but in astronomical terms, it is right outside Earth's door.

NASA, which was created by the US government in the late 1950s to explore space, sent the last **astronaut** to the Moon in 1972. The Apollo missions inspired countless young men and women to study astronomy, and NASA has remained at the center of space exploration and astronomy since that time.

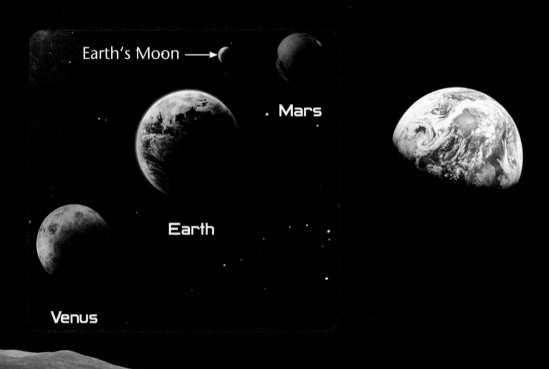

Earth's Moon ⟶

Mars

Earth

Venus

Pictures taken of Earth during NASA's Moon missions provided humans with a whole new perspective of our planet. Never before had Earth been so clearly seen as a fragile blue ball isolated in space.

NASA sends many probes into space to take pictures and gather information, including a robot called Curiosity that roams around collecting data on Mars.

Most of the men and women who do astronomy research fall into in four basic groups. Some observe. Some theorize. Some develop computer models that can organize vast amounts of data. Some build telescopes, cameras, and other electronics that help observers gather more and better information.

Computer modelers build programs that process huge amounts of observed information to predict what will likely happen next. It is similar to local weather forecasters predicting a storm by referring to computer models to determine what areas can expect bad weather.

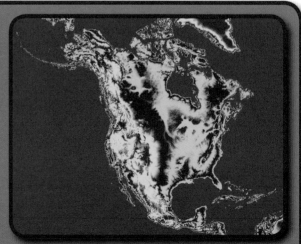

In 2012, scientists at the National Oceanic and Atmospheric Administration (NOAA) unveiled the Rapid Refresh weather model, its most modern short-term weather forecasting tool.

Powerful telescopes on Earth, as well as some that are in space orbiting beyond Earth's **atmosphere**, help observers see specific regions of space for different studies. These telescopes are in high demand because they are extremely effective and expensive to make and maintain.

The Spitzer Space Telescope operates through the Spitzer Space Center in California. The center gets so many requests from observational researchers to use the telescope that a group of astronomers has to meet to decide which projects will get to use it, and for how long.

The Spitzer telescope is designed to detect heat radiation from our own solar system to beyond the edges of our galaxy.

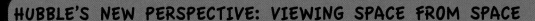

HUBBLE'S NEW PERSPECTIVE: VIEWING SPACE FROM SPACE

NASA's Hubble Space Telescope rocketed into orbit around Earth in 1990. It is the most famous of the space telescopes in part because NASA astronauts can go to it while it is in orbit and make repairs or upgrades to it. It has also provided some of the most stunning pictures of outer space.

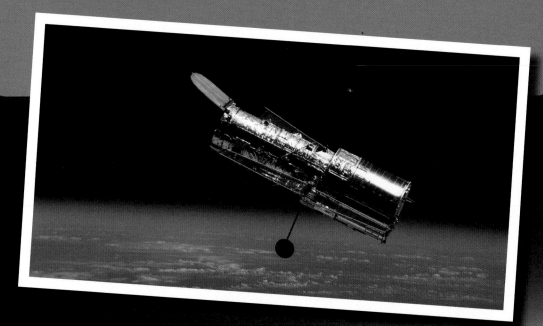

The Atmospheric Effect

Earth's atmosphere protects the planet from the Sun's ferocious heat. It also distorts what we can see of space from the planet's surface. Looking at something through the atmosphere, even using a powerful telescope, is like looking at something through a glass of water. Hubble, and the other space telescopes now in use, are outside the atmosphere, and can provide images that are not possible from telescopes on the ground.

Hubble's images include visual evidence of what astronomers say is the formation of a star from unimaginably large plumes of dust and particles deep in outer space. Space telescopes provide astronomers with a new perspective on gravity and time that previous generations of researchers did not have.

A working astronomer stays busy even though he or she may not spend more than four or five nights a year looking into a telescope. Some might never look through a telescope the way Galileo did. Researchers do a lot of writing. They write proposals for research projects and, once they conduct the research, they write about what they observed.

As in all scientific fields, astronomy research projects cost money. Researchers often write proposals about the research they want to do in order to get funding or research grants from the National Science Foundation or another source.

Astronomers at the Spitzer Space Center use **infrared** images from the Spitzer Space Telescope to document activity in dust clouds, or nebulas, from other galaxies that could be forming into distant stars.

FIELD NOTES

Astronomy is the oldest of the natural sciences. It is the only science you can't experiment with directly. You can't weigh, touch, or smell your subject matter.

The research at the Spitzer Space Center is very detailed, and provides potential clues as to how our own Sun may have formed.

Stunning images captured by the Spitzer Space Telescope show new stars heating massive dust clouds glowing red with infrared light.

Spitzer captured this image of a mysterious nebula that looks like a flaming ghost on the run. Thanks to Spitzer, astronomers can see previously hidden stars behind the pink cloud.

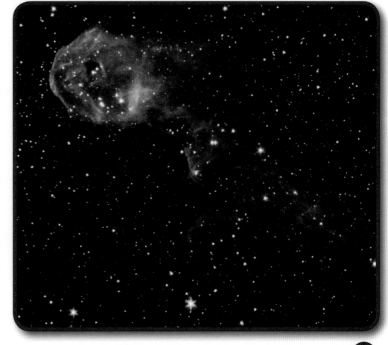

Though the day-to-day work of the professional astronomer requires a highly specialized education in physics and math, a person can use little more than their own interest in space to dabble in astronomy.

Professional astronomy research has changed with the increased complexity and capabilities of research telescopes, but many amateur astronomers still do it Galileo's way: with their own personal telescope pointed toward the sky.

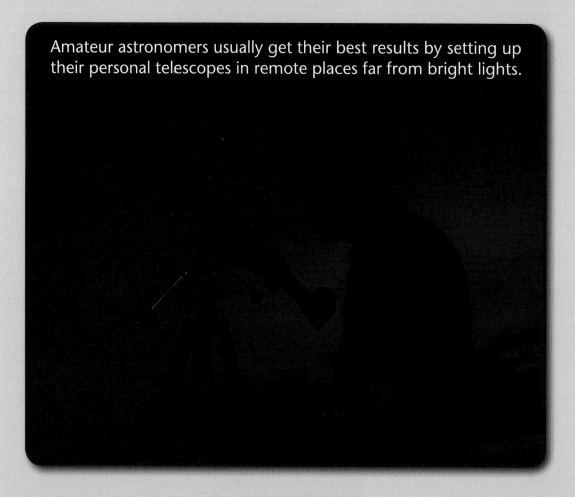

Amateur astronomers usually get their best results by setting up their personal telescopes in remote places far from bright lights.

Few physical sciences use as many amateurs to help in various fields of study as astronomy does. The amateurs, or citizen scientists, help full-time astronomers gather data, perform research, and sometimes even make important discoveries in space. Space is too massive for its study to be limited to just professionals.

Many amateur astronomers have cameras working in tandem with their telescopes. This allows them to photograph any unusual sights or activity they might observe.

CITIZEN SCIENTIST

Some programs put professionals and amateurs together on research projects.

NITARP (NASA/IPAC Teacher Archive Research Program) involves NASA partnering with teachers and students to conduct astronomy research over the course of a year.

The Cahill Center for Astronomy and Astrophysics at the California Institute of Technology (Caltech) has space for hundreds of astronomers to work together.

Astronomers at Caltech's Infrared Processing and Analysis Center (IPAC) look at the infrared images and information captured by the Spitzer Space Telescope, and organize it for research purposes.

Teachers and students help astronomers dig into data collected from telescope observation. They use computer models to map and predict activity in the nucleus of a specific galaxy deep in space. They present their findings to the American Astronomical Society, which meets each year.

Astronomy is a popular science. Each of the past two generations has had astronomers who were excellent at making the science, math, and physics of the universe not just easy to understand but fascinating as well. Carl Sagan and Neil deGrasse Tyson have made astronomy more popular with their writing, speaking, and broadcasting.

Carl Sagan (1934 -1996) hosted the astronomy TV show *Cosmos*. Here he poses with a model of a NASA spacecraft.

Neil deGrasse Tyson is an outspoken advocate for increasing government funding for NASA projects.

James Randi Educational Foundation
THE AMAZING MEETING 6
June 19-27, 2008 | Las Vegas, NV

AMAZING AMATEUR

Anthony Wesley was just doing what he loved to do, looking through his telescope in his backyard, when he noticed something odd on the planet Jupiter. He noticed a dark spot that he had never seen before on our solar system's largest planet. He took a picture of the spot and emailed it to a professional research astronomer. NASA confirmed that the image was a scar on the planet's surface left by the impact of an asteroid.

Jupiter's scar

Anthony Wesley's observation captured a rare visual clue left by an asteroid slamming into a planet. Partly by luck, he pointed his personal telescope at just the right spot, at just the right time. It gave astronomers a glimpse into a very real and frightening prospect: space objects with irregular orbits can collide with other objects, including planets.

Sometimes objects collide with Earth. The planet's atmosphere burns up nearly anything that flies into it, but in 2013 a meteorite, a small fragment of rock or metal debris from space, broke apart over Russia. The impact broke windows in buildings and left about 1,000 people injured.

Large meteoroids, or space junk, can hurtle toward Earth, but impacts are rare. Some planets, and even our Moon, are littered with craters left by impacts from meteors, suggesting they've been hit many times throughout history.

Astronomy fascinates the public. There have been countless movies, books, television shows, and even music written about outer space.

The most provocative question these stories often ask is one astronomy research has yet to answer: Is there life out there?

A newly discovered gas planet in the Milky Way galaxy, spotted by astronomers using the Spitzer Space Telescope, is among the most distant planets ever discovered. Planets beyond our own solar system are called exoplanets.

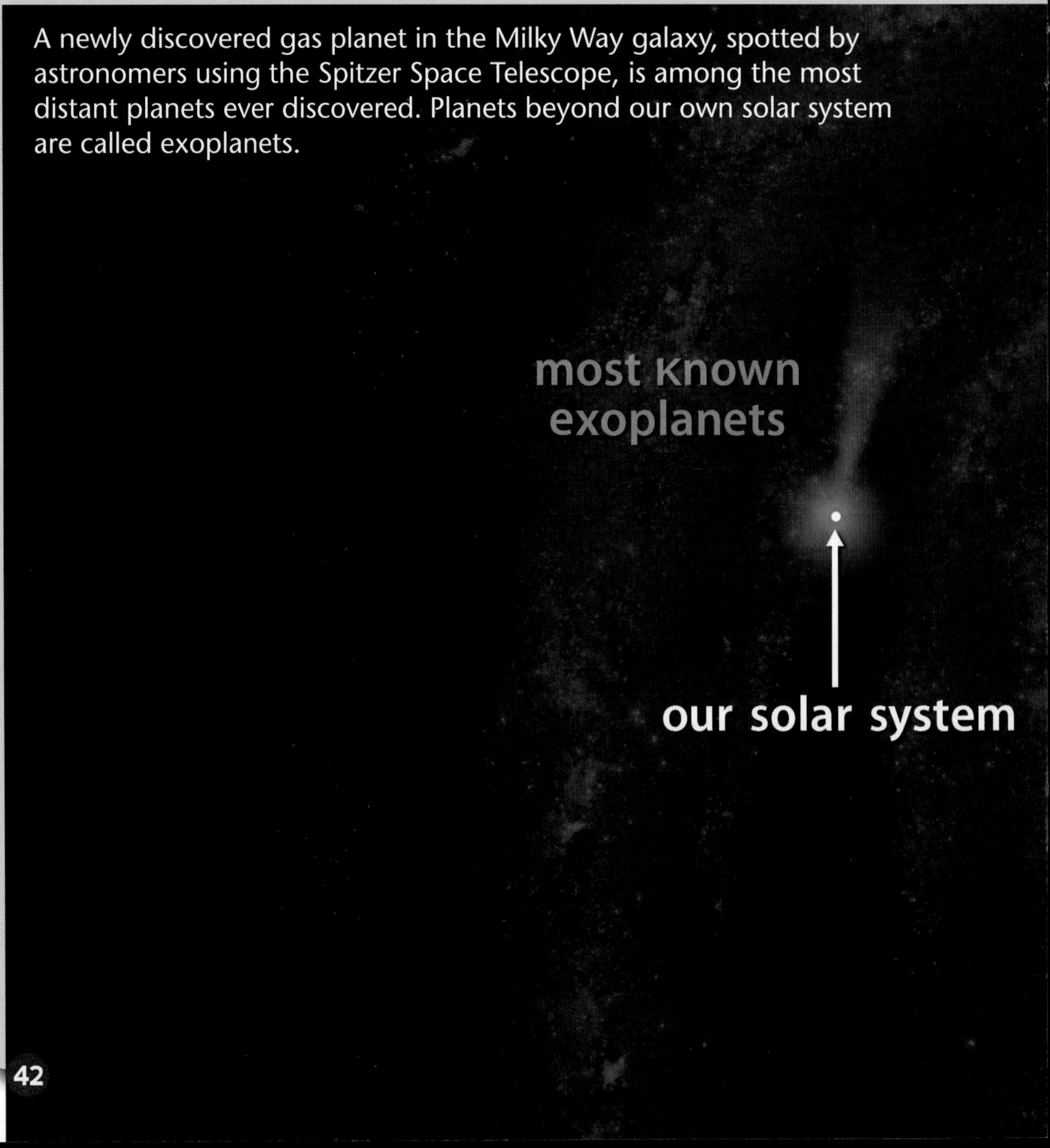

most known
exoplanets

our solar system

With so many planets orbiting around so many suns, across so many galaxies, it is fun to imagine what life on other planets might look or act like if it exists.

newfound exoplanet

MILKY WAY GALAXY

WAYS TO GET INVOLVED

You can pursue your interest in astronomy by joining a specific citizen-scientist project. Whether in science class at school, at a local planetarium, or even online, these projects can give you first-hand experience in astronomy research.

Windows2Universe.org is part of the National Earth Science Teachers Association. It offers multiple research opportunities including the Great World Wide Star Count. The online project lets students compare what they see in certain portions of the night sky with a corresponding star map. Observations are tallied online as a tool for students and scientists to mark changes over time.

The ancient Aztec civilization, in what is now Mexico, used a Sun calendar, or Sun stone, which tracked the Sun's movement to mark time.

The Hale Telescope at the Mount Wilson Observatory is considered one of the most productive in astronomical history.

TIMELINE

Ancient Times
Civilizations use the Sun's placement as a calendar.

1543
Copernicus publishes Sun-centered theory.

1609
Galileo uses telescope to observe night sky.

1656
First documented sighting of Saturn's rings.

1687
Sir Isaac Newton's theory of gravitation.

1781
French scientists observe galaxies, nebulas, star clusters.

1905
Mount Wilson Observatory established for solar study.

1914
Robert Goddard begins working with rockets.

1916
Einstein introduces Theory of Relativity.

1937
First radio telescope used.

1961
Russian Yuri Gagarin is first human in space.

1967
First pulsars, energy from dying stars, observed.

1969
American astronauts explore the Moon.

1990
NASA's Hubble Telescope launched into space.

2000
NASA probe finds evidence of water, but no life, on Mars.

2009
Amateur astronomer spots space object hitting Jupiter.

Glossary

asteroid (ASS-tuh-roid): a very small planet or object orbiting the Sun

astronaut (ASS-truh-nawt): a person who travels into space

atmosphere (AT-muhss-fihr): protective layer of gas protecting Earth

elliptical (i-LIP-tik-uhl): a imperfect circular orbit

engineering (en-juh-NIHR-ing): the designing and building of machines and structures

hypothesis (hye-POTH-uh-siss): a scientific prediction to be tested

infinite (IN-fuh-nit): never ending

infrared (in-fruh-RED): invisible energy that gives off light

irresistible (ihr-i-ZISS-tuh-buhl): unavoidable, inescapable

mathematician (math-uh-muh-TISH-uhn): a person specializing in math

observational (ob-zur-VAY-shuhn-uhl): the practice of looking at something

physical (FIZ-uh-kuhl): having to do with matter and energy

physics (FIZ-iks): the scientific study of matter and energy

Index

Show What You Know

1. Which space object was discovered as a planet but then reclassified?
2. What force helps create and maintain stars, planets, and moons?
3. Who is credited with the theory of relativity?
4. What did NASA's Apollo Mission accomplish?
5. Why are space telescope images clearer than ground-based telescopes?

Websites to Visit

www.nsf.gov/news/overviews/astronomy

www.planetary.org/explore

www.galaxyzoo.org

About the Author

Tom Greve lives in Chicago with his wife and two kids. He was born in 1969—the same year NASA first sent astronauts to explore the Moon. He has always been fascinated by the infinite distances of space, and Earth's role in the limitless universe.

Meet The Author!
www.meetREMauthors.com

www.rourkeeducationalmedia.com

PHOTO CREDITS: Cover: top photo © Aphelleon , astronomer photo © valeriopardi; page 4-5 © EpicStockMedia; page 6-7 © Blue Ice; page 8-9 © Orla; page 10-11 © John A Davis, page 10 inset © ESO/M. Kornmesser, http://www.eso.org/public/images/eso1204a/; page 12-13 © fluidworkshop (image adapted), page 13 inset photo © bikeriderlondon; page 14 horoscope © Viktoria, telescope © Triff, page 15 NASA Ames/SETI Institute/ JPL-Caltech; page 16   bottom © iryna1; page 18 inset © NASA, photographer Brian Day, page 18-19 © Image credit: NASA/JPL-Caltech; page 19; page 20-21 © Orla, page 21 inset photo courtesy of NASA; page 22 © edobric, page 23 courtesy of NASA; page 24 courtesy of NASA, Earth image © Keith Publicover, page 25 Jocelyn Bell Burnell © Astronomical Institute, Academy of Sciences of the Czech Republic; page 26 apple © Alex Staroseltsev; page 28 courtesy of NASA, page 29 inset © Vadim Sadovski, page 29 and 30 (top) photos courtesy of NASA; page 30 bottom photo courtesy of NOAA; page 31 courtesy of NASA; page 32-33 © Johan Swanepoel, hubble photo courtesy of NASA, page 33 courtesy of NASA, ESA, and the Hubble Heritage Team (STScI/AURA); page 35 Courtesy NASA/JPL-Caltech; page 36 © Sergey Kamshylin; page 37 © ChameleonsEye; page 38 © Dhilung, page 39 top courtesy of Jet Propulsion Laboratory, bottom © Napolean_70; page 40 courtesy of NASA, ESA, and the Hubble SM4 ERO Team, page 41 © Digital Storm; page 42-43 courtesy of NASA/JPL Caltech, page 43 inset © 3dmotus; page 44 sky © pixelparticle, star map © shooarts; page 45 Sun Stone © Anagoria, Observatory courtesy of NASA;

Edited by: Keli Sipperley

Cover and Interior design by: Nicola Stratford   www.nicolastratford.com

Library of Congress PCN Data

Astronomers / Tom Greve
 (Scientists in the Field)
  ISBN 978-1-63430-413-9 (hard cover)
  ISBN 978-1-63430-513-6 (soft cover)
  ISBN 978-1-63430-605-8 (e-Book)
Library of Congress Control Number: 2015931714

Also Available as:

Printed in the United States of America, North Mankato, Minnesota